INSTALL GOOGLE PLAY STORE ON YOUR FIRE

Easy Steps to Install and Use Google Play Store

BY

CHRISTOPHER C. PALMER

COPYRIGHT©2019

COPYRIGHT

TABLE OF CONTENTS

CHAPTER 1

INTRODUCTION

The Amazon Kindle Fire is an Amazon device made by Amazon and only dedicated to Amazon applications and functionalities. This is the same for both the fire tablet and fire OS. Most people using the Kindle Fire find it difficult to access most Android Applications like Facebook, WhatsApp, Gmail, Messenger, Hangout and other almost one million Apps in the Google Play Store.

Installing Google Play Store is not a very difficult procedure and will not necessarily require you rooting the Kindle Fire Tablet. With the help of this guide, this process should not take more than 30 minutes after which you can make use of the Google Play Store on your Kindle Fire device as you can on any Android device. Then you can setup and install any of your Android device launcher and convert your fire to any known Android tablet.

There are two ways you can successfully go through with this step:

1.) This step involves installing some APK files on your Device.

2.) And the second involves running the manuscript from your Windows Personal Computer (PC).

These steps are very easy due to the terms and simple nature of this work. It is designed to guide you on every step to ensure a successful Setup and installation of the Google Play Store on your Kindle Fire device and make you smile as you enjoy your device like never before.

CHAPTER 2

SETUP AND INSTALL GOOGLE PLAY STORE

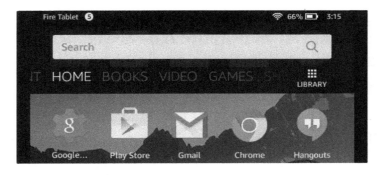

The Amazon Kindle Fire is an Amazon device made by Amazon and only dedicated to Amazon applications and functionalities. This is the same for both the fire tablet and fire OS. Most people using the Kindle Fire find it difficult to access most Android Applications like Facebook, WhatsApp, Gmail, Messenger, Hangout and other almost one million Apps in the Google Play Store.

Installing Google Play Store is not a very difficult procedure and will not necessarily require you rooting the Kindle Fire Tablet. With the help of this guide, this process should not take more than 30 minutes after which you can make use of the Google Play Store on your Kindle Fire device as you can on any Android device. Then you can setup and install any of your Android device launcher and convert your fire to any known Android tablet.

There are two ways you can successfully go through with this step:

1.) This step involves installing some APK files on your Device.
2.) And the second involves running the manuscript from your Windows Personal Computer (PC).

CHAPTER 3

INSTALL GOOGLE PLAY STORE ON APK FILE

These processes we are about to offer you have been tested severely on previous versions or models of Fire HD 8, running fire OS 5.3.1.1, and is reported to be working on the latest version 5.3.2 too, as well as the 7th Fire Tablet.

To confirm what version of Kindle Fire you are using, take the following easy steps:

Enter settings > Device options >System updates and check the version and serial number at the edge of the screen.

Let's go into the business of setting up and installing Google Play Store on your Kindle device.

First step: Download the Google play store APK file

To begin, go to settings > Security and enable "Apps from Unknown Sources". This is to permit you to install the needed APK files through which you can get the Google Play Store.

There are four APK files you will have to download, using the in-built fiber browser on your Kindle fire tablet. The easiest way to go about this is to open up this tutorial fiber browser and click the links below. This will direct you to the pages to be downloaded. They are from APK Reflection, an established and trustworthy spring for the Android APKs.

• Google Account Manager APK

• Google Services Framework APK

• Google play Services APK (use this version if you have in 2017 fire HD 8)

• Google Play store APK

In order to download each of the APK files, click on the link displayed, then scroll down, and click on "Download APK".

After clicking on download, wait as it will begin after some few seconds. After which you will see a warning notification that "this types of file can harm your device" (don't worry it won't). Click "OK" when this notification pops-up.

Repeat the same for every file that you have to download, until all four APK files are downloaded.

Second Step: Install all the downloaded Google Play Store APK Files

Exit your browser and open the folder Manager App on your Kindle Fire tablet called "Docs."

Click on "Local Storage".

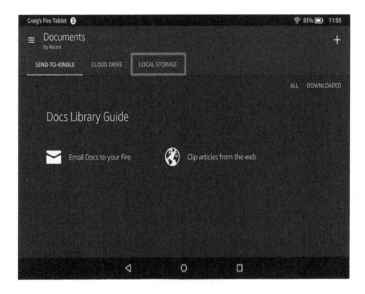

Choose the "Downloads" folder.

You will see all your APK files here on this folder.

>Click on the files start installing the App.

>Be sure to install the APK files in the order in which they where downloaded. In other words, first install the Google Account Manager APK first, then the Google Services Framework APK, followed by the Google Play Services APK and finally Google play store APK.

On the next screen display, click on "install" at the bottom to confirm installation. Toward the higher corner you will be instructed on which APK App you are installing. You must make sure that you install each of them in the correct order.

NOTE: If your "install" button fails, just switch the screen off and on, and unlock your Fire tablet files. The install button will turn from grey to orange, allowing you to continue with the installation uninterrupted.

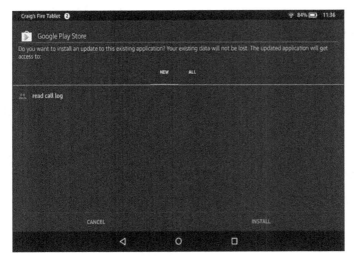

Repeat the same procedure for each of the APK files until they are all fully installed.

Third Step: Start Using Your Google Play Store

Having gone through all the processes explained above, the Google Play Store App will be displayed on the home screen of your Kindle Fire tablet. Click on it and you will be able to login with your Google account immediately.

At first this may seem not to be working properly and you may have to give it some minutes. The Google Play Store Services will automatically update themselves in the background and this may take some time.

At this point you may start searching for Apps you want and download. Some applications may request that you update your Google Play Services. If this happens, you will be directed to the Google Play Services home page where you can easily update.

CHAPTER 4

GOOGLE PLAY STORE OBJECTIVES

In case the above directive given above does not work for you for some reasons, try these complex but serviceable instructions. This has been tested on a 7th Kindle Fire Tablet and it worked well.

First Step: Prepare Your Kindle Fire Tablet

This step requires that you use a laptop and a USB cable cord for this exercise. The cable that comes with your Fire Tablet will just work fine.

On your Fire Tablet, go to settings App and click "Device options" under "Device."

Place the "serial number" field on the page. Click on it repeatedly for about seven times or more times and a "Developer Options" will appear visible below. Click "Developer Options".

Click on the "Enable ADB" option on this page to activate it. This is mainly for the developers, and you will have to agree to the warning to continue.

Once you have enabled ADB access, connect your Kindle Fire Tablet to your desktop with your USB cable. Windows would detect it and download the necessary drivers. Move to the next step – if you experience any difficulty, then you can install the Google's USB drivers manually as explained in step three of this guide.

NOTE: the process explained above might tell you to install the drivers in various ways, but the process is not advisable. It may cause you to install unsigned drivers with different packages. This is a security risk and it's impossible to go on modern 6b bit version, windows 8.1 and windows 10 without restarting and disabling driver signature verification. All this might happen automatically and make you think this guide is out of date.

CHAPTER 5

SETUP AND INSTALL GOOGLE PLAY STORE FROM YOUR PC?

This would enable you download some Apps in APK form and install them. If you do this regardless you may still need to make use of ADB command to set up permission on at least one of the Apps. Instead of doing this the long way, we will be using a manual that installs the Apps and sets up the permissions for you automatically.

On your PC, go to the underground junky website and download the "Amazon -Fire 5th - Gen- Install-Play Store zip file." Extract or unzip or move the contents of the zip file to another folder on your computer. Double the tap"1-install play store.bat" file to begin with it.

Unlock the Kindle fire tablet and agree to "Allow USB debugging". If this does not appear, close the command prompt window and re-launch the bat file above again.

On the first screen, "type 2" and click enter to have the tool install the Google Play Store.

The suitable drivers will have to be installed for this of course. But, if you see "Allow USB debugging" option on your Fire tablet agree to it, then you will know the drivers are working well.

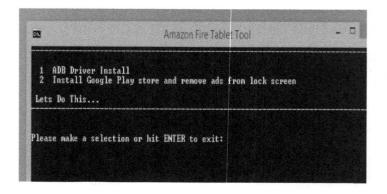

The requested package will be installed on your connected Fire tablet, including Google Play Services and the Google Play Store App.

Restart your fire tablet when requested to do so.

Hold the power button for a while, click "OK" when you are asked if you need to shut it down, and then switch it on again.

Unplug the fire tablet from your computer now and possibly disable the "enable ADB" option you enabled earlier.

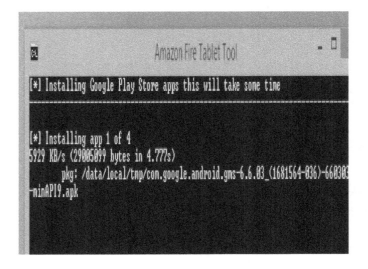

Third Step: Utilize the Google Play store

After restarting, you will find the Play Store and Google settings shortcuts on your fire's home screen. Click on "play Store" and you can sign in with an existing Google account or create a new one.

It may not work normally at first after you sign in, give it some minutes. The Google play store and Google play services will automatically update themselves in the background. This may take about ten minutes.

You can now search Google Store and install Google Apps like Gmail and Chrome that aren't available on Amazon app store. Any Android App from the Google play Store should work.

Some Apps may ask that you update Google Play Services. If this is the case you will be directed to the Google Play Services page in Google Play. Where you can also update Google play Services with a single click on the button.

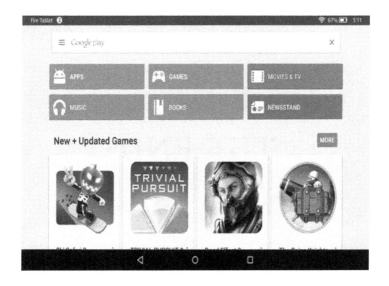

APPRECIATION

Appreciations go to the XDA developer forum for writing some of these methods, and underground junky for their scripts. If you need some troubleshooting help or you'd like to do it manually without a script, edge over to the XDA- developers forum seek for more information.

THE END